BLOOD
ARIA

WISCONSIN POETRY SERIES

Edited by Ronald Wallace and Sean Bishop

CHRISTOPHER NELSON

BLOOD ARIA

THE UNIVERSITY OF WISCONSIN PRESS

Publication of this book has been made possible, in part, through support from the Brittingham Trust.

The University of Wisconsin Press
728 State Street, Suite 443
Madison, Wisconsin 53706
uwpress.wisc.edu

Gray's Inn House, 127 Clerkenwell Road
London EC1R 5DB, United Kingdom
eurospanbookstore.com

Printed in the United States of America
This book may be available in a digital edition.

Library of Congress Cataloging-in-Publication Data
Names: Nelson, Christopher (poet), author.
Title: Blood aria / Christopher Nelson.
Other titles: Wisconsin poetry series.
Description: Madison, Wisconsin : The University of Wisconsin
          Press, [2021] | Series: Wisconsin poetry series
Identifiers: LCCN 2020036113 | ISBN 9780299331542 (paperback)
Subjects: LCGFT: Poetry.
Classification: LCC PS3614.E44537 B56 2021 | DDC 811/.6—dc23
LC record available at https://lccn.loc.gov/2020036113

CONTENTS

BLOOD ARIA

A DEDICATION

To you of the unimaginable
tomorrow, we loved as you will love

as you will find it a way to
endure this banishment

into the singular island of a body
that will be gently

worn to failure, like a solid pier
by the touch of waves

which regard their work as
constant encouragement. To you

for whom these words will be
quaint and lacking

the magnitude of your vibrant
now, it is night for me.

I open the window despite
January to hear the voices

of the few passersby
stolen by wind and smothered

by the rush of cars.
Gas is $2.79 a gallon and I

am forty-three years. Carlos is lost.
Shayma and Sharif unable to return.

Jacob, Michael, Gabe, Juanita,
Blas. I still see Sky,

before the bullet un-
wound time, the pink hat she wore

that Tuesday in the rain.

COCK FIGHT

Being, as a general rule, left-handed, the blade is fitted
    to the right claw of the largest rooster to counterbalance
    the benefit of its greater strength, and the higher jumper
    gets a half-inch blade instead of the usual three-quarters:
    death and the desire for symmetry

through asymmetry. The Romans employed similar methods
    in the Colosseum: a man advantaged by horseback
    wore a blackout helmet; a frail prisoner struggled
    with a heavy sword while his Herculean opponent
    wielded a shield small as a salad plate.

When I was younger, identity and sexuality were more
    ensnared, and discrepancies in physicality heightened arousal:
    a swollen phallus beside a limp inferior, a six-foot athlete
    and a scrawny boy surrendering to him on the carpet.
    As one ages, a paradox becomes familiar:

the increased distance between present and past may not weaken
    the influence of what was: a child still resides inside
    the wrinkling man; a child still runs through pastures,
    nearly convinced that belief alone can make him soar,
    so thin is the separation between dream and non-dream.

Isn't the acceptance that there is such a thing as non-dream
    what marks the descent into adulthood? Before battle
    the cocks are made furious by a lesser bird called
    "the monkey," then they fight—leaping and fluttering,
    feathers flaring, ebony, emerald, and rust—until one dies.

In the golden eyes, bewitching calm. When I was ten or eleven,
    an errand sent me to the high school, a mission of retrieval,
    a folder for a teacher. There was a "secret" landing
    at the top of the stairs by the unused dance studio,
    a six-by-ten-foot sanctuary for those who cut class.

My wrong turn led me there, where I watched, unnoticed
      for half a minute, four boys—two I recognized from
      the wrestling team—flaps of blue jeans opened, shirts
      half removed or pulled up and held in teeth, tanned torsos,
      taut nipples, tight curls from navels down to the red rods

being thrummed as one counted *twenty-three, twenty-four,*
      twenty-five—a contest: who can come the quickest—
      twenty-six, twenty-seven, twenty-eight and the pearlescent
      spit from one, the others surprised by the speed—
      flushed cheeks and *Jesus*, a soft exclamation.

One saw me then, and he fixed my eyes with a fierce intensity,
      not anger or desire, not fear or shame, but perhaps
      some feeling that contained all of these. Their age
      and audacity granted them power over me.
      I fled, returned without the folder,

said I couldn't find it, and nothing else was asked. So this is a story about
      introjection, the imprinting of consciousness by events
      charged with symbolic force. I don't know how many times
      I've revisited the top of the stairs in my mind.
      Like all birds, the cock has little blood, but a bleeding wound

won't make them stop, the desire to fight not quelled by injury;
      instead the organism persists in its aggression until
      failure, death-lust still active when the body
      is unable to respond. In high school I had a secret lover.
      When he would enter me, what I marveled at most was how

who I was—or thought I was—would fade,
      a much easier way to lose the self, I used to muse,
      than crawling for miles on hands and knees,
      like the pilgrims I read about, to a holy altar, where,
      in the body's exhausted distress, what seems to be

—and may in fact be—the soul leans outward, through the eyes,
   toward the material. I was wrong, my metaphor incomplete.
   Maybe an erasure of and a heightening of the sense of self
   have the same outcome. As the blade is affixed to the foot,
   the master will whisper, and the cock feels not the meaning

of the words but its god's desire. It has been said that
   the contest is not between the birds but the souls
   of their keepers. And some day, too, I will realize
   that this extended comparison I've been making
   also fails, as when a young man, who seeks

in the bodies of others the virility possessed in his own,
   comes to know that he is and is not his father
   —image of two teetering scales—as he erroneously
   believes that in coming there is a kind of knowing,
   so he comes and comes and comes, as we all do—or did—

for our various reasons, in our various seasons, watched over,
   we might sense, by an intelligence there is no name for—
   like the roosters, the audience invisible to them, beyond
   their cognition, despite the necessity of its presence
   in the bloodletting that defines them.

THE BLOND BOMBER

Not Billy Walker, the English heavyweight boxer, not
　　a B-17 rumbling toward Dresden, its sexy
　　bare-bottomed mascot smiling, but the boy

down the street who taught me to play knucklebones
　　the summer he returned from New Zealand with
　　a set of plastic knobby things made to resemble

the actual. He could do *thread the needle* and *horse
in the stable* while I'd get stumped by *little jingles.*
　　"Bomber" because, according to gossip, he could

ejaculate seven feet, the sort of thing boys ascribe power to,
　　but he also batted cleanup, dated Amanda Prince,
　　held the record for the 400 meter, and had

a T-shirt signed by Ozzy Osborne, so taken together, he was
　　better than you and me. The day we convinced him
　　to show us, in the treehouse in the box elder,

late afternoon sunlight slanting in, our faces bright
　　on one side, shadow the other, was also the day
　　his father would fall from a roof while shingling

and impale himself on rebar. I saw him today, after twenty-
　　something years, at the Qwik Mart, built where
　　the ballfield had been. We shook hands, said little,

fidgeted like shy boys—he, overweight and bald,
　　buying low-sodium pretzels, and I still watching
　　in the treehouse that no longer exists.

CAPITAL CITY AT MIDNIGHT

I want to write about empowerment and newfound freedoms,
    but this is the poisoned poem in my heart tonight.
    In a car parked in an alley, three men wait: a tire iron,
    a towing chain, a baseball bat. Last year there were
    1,200 known hate crimes against gays in America,

but the data is incomplete because twenty states don't include
    sexual orientation in their hate-crimes laws. Incomplete
    because of underreporting and a tradition of fear
    and shame. After the club closes a thirty-six-year-old
    accountant will walk home with a new contact in his phone.

He will survive, but his ribs will need wired together,
    half his jaw replaced with bovine bone
    and titanium screws, and two years of therapy
    will help him accept, to a degree, what he's lost.
    I know one of the perpetrators—high school, a semester

of P.E.—who will be arrested on a fluke: a passerby will recall
    three numbers from the license plate because they match
    his ex-lover's birthday. And coincident: a boy this night
    hangs himself with a belt from the shower spigot.
    His parents told him, after he came out, he doesn't belong

in their home. A common story. His name is Cody, a gymnast
    aspiring to be a pediatric nurse. Is there room for him
    in your memory? *Capital City at Midnight* is the title
    of an ink and watercolor painting by a friend
    who became sick and died from AIDS. It depicts

a monolithic, translucent cowboy boot through which is seen
    a skyscraper, where men silhouetted in lit windows
    contemplate their place in the order. I was a boy,
    the first light tufts in my pubis and pits. He visited
    my parents, effusive and gestural, with an exotic toy dog.

I wrote him a poem called "June Moon," of which I remember
        some lines: something about nighthawks cooing
        in the trees, "tulip wish, two lips kiss . . . baby maybe
        love me long." Years pass. I'm home from college,
        summer break. He earned millions as a Hollywood

designer and bought an historic Mormon manor, where,
        to the chagrin of the community, he hosts outrageous
        parties. At two a.m., the background din of a house filled
        with conversation, music, and laughter—a moment,
        the two of us alone. I see in him the first

suggestions of disease, loss of weight, quieter. His whitening
        bristles on my neck as he kisses me where no grown man
        has yet kissed. He whispers that he loves me, and I feel
        pitiful to be the object of a dying man's affection.
        And how absurd—he hardly knows me—

and how true. In his field is a Shetland pony named Petunia.
        Children used to stop by to feed her apples
        and honey clover through the rail fence, before
        their parents forbade it, before they were told
        this is a place to fear. She has walked toward us.

I see her light shape faintly in the dark. Not knowing
        how to respond to his advance, I ask why
        he named her Petunia. He says, "I didn't.
        She came with the house. Poor lonely girl,
        I think she knows she'll be dog food before her time."

That winter I replicated his painting. I decorated the giant
        see-through boot with gilding pigments and a lone
        star. I was the one in the skyscraper window. I was blue,
        and true to life, I couldn't make myself match
        my idea of a man. There was a car parked in the alley,

the two red beads of its brake lights, three shadows waiting inside.
And hovering above it all, a moon that I spent too much
time on, favoring the fantasy of it, transforming it
into a Ferris wheel and then God's bad eye.

SPECULATIONS ON MY CONCEPTION

The soft rumble of the water heater reheating as my parents
       share a bath. The discomfort of cramped knees
       trumped by small intimacies: lavender bath salt, luffa
       along the back, incense sending up a white brushstroke
       from the potted fern, him frothing her hair with shampoo,
       his partial erection buoyant. September 1974.

Or was it a night of boxing and beer, Howard Cosell's voice rising
       with the frenzy of the strikes as he works his fingers
       into her jeans, their first two sons finally in bed?
       And does it matter?

Shamans say the mood of the conception colors the entire life.
       Him lowering into her, lifting and lowering, the familiar
       room made dreamlike by the drug of fucking,
       the distance from bed to mirror somehow different,
       the glow of the lamp warmer, then
       him giving in to the personal violence of coming.

Schefflera, stained glass, two-foot candle brought back
       from Vietnam carved with glyphs. The end
       of summer, my young mother thinking already of
       baby names: Sasha, Sarah, Stephanie.

Three months later, womb-dreaming, breathing mother-blood,
       small as your thumb at page's edge, what-will-become-a-boy
       experiencing its first color—or not a color
       but the perception of darkness, the foveal jelly eye
       sealed, so many years yet for light.
       And we can hope—should hope—

that where cells agree to shape a mouth, one day there will be
       singing and sun-warmed sugar peas from a garden
       the child will help sow. Before blizzards
       quell the sentimental
       and cancer enforces the code.

THE HOUSE WHERE FATHER HAS GONE TO DIE

is spartan and small, and the trees look like they were drawn
    by a five-year-old.
    Predictable how the limbs resemble
    reaching arms.

He's walking beneath them, his hand on the bark as if
    remembering the texture will be important
    where he is going,
    as if it might be possible
    to remember after all.

I'm at the breakfast table, bewildered by a stack of bills:
    dermatologist, oncologist, radiologist, three surgeons.
    ... As if drawn with charcoal or crayon, a facsimile of
    an idea of
    a memory of *tree.*

He's at the spruce where once he showed me wooly aphids
    webbing the fresh lime-green buds with eggs,
    and later, when that soft newness had turned
    rusty and gnarled
    into spiky armored wombs,

winged adults emerged, complete and somehow already ready
    for the world. Forgive my nostalgia
    and metaphors, but sometimes
    we shouldn't be ashamed

to use the handholds. His house is clean and tidy,
    as it's always been, and I wonder about that,
    how habits last
    and what security they might provide,
    some hex against inevitable transformation.

He makes his way back, past the poppy patch, which
  occupies one-third of the yard, a veritable
  madness of beauty
  for a few days each May. He reports on

the heron fishing the shallows of the marsh
  by the river behind the house and through
  the alfalfa field, which will be cut
  any day now—and can I smell it,
  the rich tea-like aroma, grassy and full

of his fifty-eight summers? *That's too young,*
  everyone at the funeral will say.
  ... Or perhaps the trees
  look like they've been drawn
  to replace actual trees because

actual trees are part of the actual world,
  which can no longer be—my child
  mind fears—without him in it.
  Child mind still present
  despite my own

decades of involvement in the dance,
  the play, the largely
  banal sacrament of
  passing
  one day to the next.

ON PATERNITY

Coquettish the "policeman"
then lewd with his black baton—
because the purpose of Halloween
is to forget
the parameters you've made a life of.
When my drunken father threw
the ghost across the kitchen
and a boy was loosed
from the sheet, he learned
that masks fail
not from temporariness
but their too-accurate show
of what is wanted. The ghost's longing
for nothing more
than to choose
when the invisibility so familiar
could be a cloak
or could be wished away
with a single word, like *hello*,
given, of course, courage,
which every ghost story requires.
Now the ghost is twenty-five
at a nightclub, where other ghosts
are coifed and shaven
and expensively adorned
in hope
that a living eye might regard them.
But the flashing televisions, the paid
dancers—how obvious the futility
to compete. When the boy
could stand, he saw that the scattered
medallions of chocolate and the feckless
variety of sweets now meant less
than any imaginable thing.
And if the mask is fire,
get used to saying *goodbye*,

and if the mask weren't
riveted in place, what's before him
wouldn't be
so arresting now.

JULY

through locker room windows light the color of lemonade

    from the pool children's squeals

and I'm doing what I'm supposed to: not looking

    at the naked boys and men

even in here there's a television: girl in the hairspray commercial

    urges *touch it, touch it, touch it*

    because it will hold

THIS TIME THISTLES

certain things that happen
you don't you can't come back from

we know this we fear this yet we
move toward their possibility (bell

in a fog) with vague longing or
(razor in the lace drawer)

irrational dread
when I was six the nine-year-olds

fucked me with their dicks smaller
than grown men's thumbs one after

the other (why do we love lord)
and the vault door

slammed trapping ~~a panic a lust~~ a panic
that's never gone away (qué será será)

how this year the thistles took
the field and last year it was

wild yarrow thousands of lacy
landing pads for the still unnamed

flies and mimic bees who
make a meal of those few drops

ARS POETICA

in the little red journal you've kept
since puberty chronicling your ten thousand shames
which you whisper while you sleep
a plastic statuette of Don Quixote your only auditor
his face lucid and crazed
unchanging eyes open against the darkness
no wind moving the windmill
no wind when you write *the spinning blades of the mill*
in the little red journal that exists
even after it hisses in the fire

ON PATERNITY

eighteen and sharp in the brushed olive wool of a cadet
on leave. Summer, sixty-five years before
dying. Spears of late lilac and he holds

●

kaleidoscopic the mind loosens itself
from the body husk, body shell, coat
of 330 seasons. He holds his cap

●

spears of lilac wasting in the humble
parlor of a railroad man, waiting for
the daughter to join him for a milkshake and

●

the future. I, a possibility within
a possibility: the wig in the sprig
burrowed deep and drunk

HALLUCINATION WITH FOUR FATHERS

Late November, sky the color of brushed steel and as cold.
A wood-paneled sedan spins in the mud, and my father swears
at eternity for every injustice done to him. It is thirty-five
years ago and he is thirty-five, and he spins and rocks
the idiot machine forward and back, blue smoke
circling up from the left rear tire as I stand
over his grave, where he is a few handfuls of ash
in a cup, in a box, in a blackness thick as thirty-
five years of night in which he sleeps off a weekend drunk
in a room cologned by his body. Stuck in the muck,
car full of kids, their faces stare from fogged windows
at the pitiless strategies of winter, his curses audible
between the engine's tired revs. My father trots toward them,
signals that he will push, leans his weight into the cold metal
                              and just like that, they are free.

GEMINGA

My dead father is singing in the shower.
Our past unresolved, so he continues to sing

as steam seeps beneath the bathroom door.
I mistook his anger for a lack of love

and for this reason I have a penurious heart.
Evening interstate crossed by coyotes

come to lick a restaurant's trough of grease.
Mother bleaches her teacups.

Mother on the porch swing (light in the birch)
kissing a new man, kissing a new man.

And then we're here again, in the kingdom
misnamed *the past*. Father undoes

the sash of her blue robe. He's impossibly
engorged and sees me watching from the threshold.

What came before this I don't recall, but we're climbing
the ancient pine to see who can reach

the highest branches—Father and me.
We come to a place of unsure footing,

houses below so small, as if I had mistaken
a diorama for the world, sunlight (brighter here)

on my face, which is also his. . . . Wait—
all these years I've lied: Father is high in the tree

and I watch from below, afraid to join him,
not because of height but the desire

to jump. I don't know why he climbs or why
the only sound is his laughter. Memory,

the sprung clock. Mother's eye blackened by him
but once, yet it continues to steal my attention.

Even as a child I was skeptical of prayer,
but I used to pray for her, in my way. And now?

For Father, for Mother, for Lover, for Other—
all comprise my Geminga,

decayed core of a massive star, exploded
and invisible to naked vision—

there but not there: the silence I listen to
as an act of praise.

ELEGY FOR A RIVER

(Dry Delta of the Colorado)

The array of rectangular tailings ponds
    (chemical and mineral detritus)
    seen from the air
    can be made by the imagination
    into a fallen mythic bird

of impure jade, andalusite, fire
    opal, and tourmaline
    held in cohesion in cloisonné,
    a massive elegant wing
    smothering
    what could be a village
    in this gray waste

where children gather at fence lines
    and whisper confessions
    of how their fathers
    hold them
    at night when
    thunder crawls through
    their minds
    rendering them

the smallest of small things, bird food in a dream
    of horrible songs.
    But no,
    this is the pus of earth,
    wounded mother
    coagulation
    gathered and employed.

Matter and *mother* share a linguistic root;
    father and *feather*
    do not.

Once, as a child, he and I watched
     a badelynge of ducks
     frozen
     in lake ice.
     We looked at them from the cold shore
     through field glasses,
     which we passed between us,
     our talisman of
     togetherness,

the ducks calling,
     shrill, baffled and echoless.
     I wanted to walk out to the freeze
     and free them,
     but you said the ice wouldn't hold.

Funny what stays in memory:
     I rarely think of the ducks and their dying,
     but the quiet
     resigned and certain tone
     in which you would speak—
     I wake from it now and again.

When last I visited the cemetery where
     you're buried, it took awhile
     to locate your stone.
     Stepping among the faded
     and fallen Memorial Day wreaths,
     checking the nearby trees and houses
     against memory
     and marveling

at how they didn't match, how I had
     imagined you to be
     further
     from the road,
     how certainties
     can derail us. As in,

"You never came to me in the night."

But I intended to say something about
        the relationship
        between responsibility and imagination:
        it matters
        that art not be yet another
        bright
        escape hatch

from the irreparable things
        we have done. We have to
        sit
        in the toxic dross
        and let it
        burn
        everything
        away

until all that is left of our important thoughts
        is a silence
        beyond adjectives.

CHILDHOOD

your girlfriend wears her summer
dress and the music
is loud and you don't care about the bruises
because this is being alive

the chrysanthemums you picked are
one full day from collapse
when she brings her mouth to yours
yes and yes and yes

because this is happiness
there is no evening
downpour
and in Father's car

the alternator doesn't fail
and the miles you would have had to walk
aren't dark and fraught
with what you hope are birds

SEASCAPE WITH THE SEA ERASED

A horizon to relegate you
to the denominator. What is above

sears and enlightens and will take you
into itself

without remainder. The pier is
a simple umber taper

scratched horizontally for the illusion
of light through boardwalk

boardwalk for allusion
to the first summer

fondle and how forgotten
the incoming waves

MIDLIFE

winsome we were we rushed to catch
the first flirt the first fire

the childhood provoked
exuded a juice resembling milk
until the spate was spent

now the head so heavy the hands that hold it
press into the eyes
so what is seen is seen double

lamp in night window
now twin lights

the man wearing two faces
now four faced
and each of them you

FIDELITY

Night comes first to the innermost
branches of the elm, then hedgerows, then entire lawns.

My neighbor gets ready for bed, her one lit window and the red pulse

of a radio tower above the bay. Our backyards are small
and touch each other along one side.

MÖBIUS STRIP

Behind the curtains,
a world. Behind the breast-
bone, a clock carefully wired.

I only wanted to be
perfect. Is that transgression
forgivable? No,

I also wanted you
in the light of the window seat
wearing the robe that falls away,

you who asked why I believe
I can turn from love
and not be destroyed,

you who said my eyes—
it was autumn and is it not possible
to return?

Behind the shoulder blade,
a lung. Behind identity, a shard
                              of God.

LITTLE OCHRE FLAME

1

In the autumn courtyard of the cathedral of San Felipe
    angled light on lovers holding each other
    in a pact that can easily exclude them.
Light on compass cactus, light on bee-smothered mesquite
    blooming unseasonably
    because of parasitizing mistletoe.
Light on fish in the fabricated pool, flashing
    where sun touches them
    between snake reed and flat leaf.

Now that my breakdown has ended, I see how people can be reborn.
    It takes time, and what I was
    is the only obstacle. The choir singing inside,
somehow childlike in their white and red robes
    as hexagonal light from stained glass
    bathes them and bathes
the bronze crucifix and its hierarchic face of anguish.
    I think of how the Romans punished variously,
    how tax evaders were roped to a pole

low enough that goats could lick their bare feet—
    rough pink and black tongues—
    and each afternoon, with a bucket of brine
bearing an insignia of empire, a man would
    brush the raw feet
    so when the goats where brought
on their hemp tethers, they would lick the salt
    until the skin came away.
    Inside they are singing

the parable of the mustard seed—
    how Jesus said that even faith so small
    can accomplish the impossible,
that what no one needs is more faith.
    The old baritones' jowls are shaking,
    their seasoned voices, thick as lather
or winter honey in a kitchen where an estranged husband
    watches the silent snow, moment
    upon moment, cover the gazebo

where once the pact was affirmed.
    (That's my fear of aloneness showing through:
    a little ochre flame to havoc my imagination.)
One drums his fingers on the pew, one closes his eyes
    as the crescendo happens inside him.
    Wednesday the pumpkin vendor will spread his harvest,
and we will buy some, as we do each year,
    and you will cut the most beautiful face
    and I the most awful, and we will watch

what we have created
    manifest by the light we put inside them.

2

When one is being reborn, one doesn't ask,
    Where is God?

The tulip decaying on its stalk,
    the papery crimson beacon becoming

flaccid and pale—God is there, in the rot.
    Ultimate otherness residing everywhere, but

accessible only if I can love myself.
    Thank You, Lord, for that challenge.

The statue in the plaza of San Felipe is a goat.
    God gives us simple needs: thirst—

to taste the salt, to taste the sun
    in the unmown grass, to taste

the god in the blood.
    Isn't that the official recommendation?

3

Might they have a counterpart in the 21st century, those ten virgins,
five of whom prepared to surrender
    in bondage to a man,
    five out looking for lamp oil?

When the second five arrive late, the night banquet underway,
at the door in the light of their own lamps,
    they are unrecognized
    and sent away. An allegory

encouraging preparedness and faith; our futures assured,
but under what conditions? What readiness
    could a soul need—
    soul, that which we still can't define?

Aren't we all impeccable in essence? At the shopping mall,
four hundred shades of makeup:
    for every girl the possibility
    of a more perfect mask.

She wakes to birds and returns to dreams but brokenly.
There might or might not be a man,
    a fact that matters, but does it matter less
    in this century?

(Cue history's parade—its gory glory, its tedium.)
That her face be perfected for a man—
     a face that, we are assured,
     in its ugly nudity

is like God's. Or: a face that *is* God's, as is yours.
And what had they learned, the disciples, so eager
     in their questions,
     so needful of reassurance?

When will the world end? When will we be with You in paradise?
The afterlife was yesterday; the beforelife, tomorrow.

4

The young man and woman picnicking beneath the bamboo
are in love. I can tell by how serious is their playfulness.

Only in courtship does the frivolous determine the future—
perhaps also in academia, politics, and war:
     the women whose children are still alive
     string laundry from claws of rebar; those without
     take their bitterness inward and wither.

But the lovers are far away—olives, cubed cheese, a baguette,
sparkling wine. What he doesn't tell her—
     he's had two hundred lovers—
     is what he tries to excuse
     from his identity.

And she enjoys feeling again and feeling unknown to herself.
A black helicopter chops apart the quiet, but they don't hear it;

they're in another dream, the one where God is squeezed
from the lover's body—born in scream and blood to become
    more, or other,
    or another,
    or a me or you.

Sometimes the bed sheets, when gathered from the rebar claw,
are shot through. It is only better to be among the living because
    one day
    we will have to say goodbye,
    and sometimes that makes us act accordingly.

5

When the drumline practices in the sun—
    cymbals flashing and the synchronized
    motions of their arms
    mismatch the sound at this distance—
    the young men occasionally
    remove their shirts, and I come to watch,
    their taut arms, the wide coins of their nipples
    to purchase my eyes.
And what of it, desire? To what end? No end—don't I see?
    To *not* end. Everything moves
    forward on this fuel.
When you approach the horizon, it will not recede,
    but you will
    never reach it—
    and that too is a metaphor for God.

6

It is possible, is it not, God, that I matter? For I've had to
    destroy them
    so that I can live
—countless chickens, cows, carrots, fish, broccoli, potatoes—
so that I can continue
    to imagine that I'm consulting You with these words.

My lover reads them—after the shower, her hair in a wet braid,
gravity pulling the water
    to the curled tip
where her blouse is dampened. She rises, she goes
    to throw seeds to the towhees
    and cardinals. A cry—the blue hawk

returns to the tree and sends the little birds into panic,
    like gunfire might
    to me and you, reader,
who recycles these words that once were my mind
    —and still may be—
    and are now yours.

And You? Weren't they always Yours?
    Sometimes the hawk
    —if only I could be half as confident—
catches a dove in flight. It eats, the yard silent and wholly its own,
    so that it can continue
    to be what it is

because what it is is more important than
    what the dove was,
    simply by claiming itself so.
Is this Your model? Is it in this way we are like You?
    Can it be otherwise?
    Are there paradigms

to which even You are bound? If I refuse this *way*,
    this predation,
    will I be closer to You?
    Will I be *less* You?

7

Awake at three a.m., heart hammering, in a panic
    of identity. How could I have been
    for all these years
    who I was so convinced I was?
    And how could I—suddenly—
    not be that? And if I'm not, who am I?
Outside, no solace. The occasional traffic freighting
    its countless possibilities.
    Where are they going
    and from what
    at this hour
    and so fast and how easily
    the body breaks? Night traveler,
be safe. I can't be unaware of the danger of your late errand,
    the lover's wetness still inside you,
    your blood-alcohol too high.
    How the lines blur,
    the feeble lines that can't
    hold
    the throttling steel and light.
    How the stolid tree
    uproots slightly and tilts
    as the car
    and the living mind inside
    fold
    origami-like into some exotic bloom.

Even water is difficult to swallow—some wild terror upon me—
    and to recognize how maudlin,
    this only worsens the despair.
There, at the birdbath, a fox stands to drink,
    and it feels my watching;
    it turns, it tries to discern
    my form in the darkness,
    rejects my pointlessness,
    drinks more
    then leaps
    onto the wall and runs its length into the brambles
    of the undeveloped quarter acre.

8

Late October, now invisible are the millipedes and spiders,
the geckos and skinks, night jars, tanagers, and swifts.
The moon rises in partial eclipse—Hunter Moon, the calendar says—
a flattened red oblong over the coruscating city.
Why would someone walk into darkness, into this cactus forest
with an intention and a saw, and set upon a forty-foot saguaro?
Now toppled, freshly, the waxy expandable sides still firm
and sage green, the woody ribs sheared, revealing the symmetrical
star-shape of its ancient inside, sponge-like, silent, and, yes, wise.
And what am I doing alone in this place called by so many
forsaken, where I walk accompanied by self-doubt,
unlike one training to see God? God, who emerged from
some first darkness then invented for us an experience that begins
with an emergence into blood, noise, hunger, and pain—
I'm tempted to claim that compassion must be manmade.
Perhaps You've sent us here to revise what You are.
We call it Hunter Moon—as in moon by which to hunt? Moon
in whose light we are hunted? Are made hunters? Are mine
the teeth of a hunter? This one in my lower jaw, cracked,
split to the pulp, so that hot drink or an open-mouth breath
cause me to wince—a reminder: *I too am already involved*

in the rot. Tonight in a dream, in a mirror (a face mostly mine)
with a spring-loaded miniature hammer, fussing to be rid of it,
rid of you, little tooth. How when I wake, you will win my attention
all day, and I will touch you, repeatedly, like a lover, with Our tongue.

9

Consider the ravens, for they neither sow nor reap,
which have neither storehouse nor barn; and God feeds them.
Of how much more value are you than the birds?
—LUKE 12:24

The keepsake in her hand—small as a tortoise just hatched
and going forth cautiously but already compelled
        by the single need that won't cease driving it
        until the only greater dictum intervenes.

Autumn light, recent rain, perfume of mesquite and acacia—
she whispers, *my first child.* She came home at the usual time,
        put the keys in the bowl, saw him
        in the bathtub pale and shaking,

wrist veins hacked open with a mezzaluna.
The second child, a girl barely walking, sat on the sun-warmed
        concrete (April, lilac)—she says it's still impossible
        to comprehend that it happened—

and the husband backed over her in the Ford.
Now (crow's feet, tangle of gray) she says, fingers tracing invisible
        shapes on my shoulder,
        I'm ready to have another.

So resumes the larger narrative. Her sheets smell of lavender,
and I'm suspicious of how it will end.
        But I've lived long enough
        to not trust suspicions.

And so I say *okay*, and they come back—how many years now?—
the small tears. Is it happiness
    or the surprise that I am again
    what I didn't think I would be?

Luke's riddle of value. So much in the storehouse taken by mold.
So much in the field that will never be sold.

IMBOLC

in love and therefore
uncostumed we
are again holding
each other in the steady but ultimately
frail architecture of our bodies
the first costume
we had no role in choosing
or maybe we did but
I don't recall doing so do you
in some unembodied beforelife craving
this world of noise and pain
and temporary pleasure this single
berry I give to you from winter
cracked fingers one red temple
of seeds and sun
shuttled all the way around this earth for
our two moments of joy
of which we must believe
ourselves worthy

SEDUCTION

1

if I imagine God I merely imagine
but with what other apparatus are we to engage?
it might happen with age a further necessity
to believe as we sometimes see
a sudden conflagration in the corn

2

all things carry a quantity of fire
to accomplish nothing but their own promulgation:
how the peacock's tail changes color as it turns
how some swans intended to be black
how even a glance can't be taken back

THE BORROWED WORLD

(Matthew 21:33–46)

1

Late sun in the grapes, black grapes on the trellised vines,
    heavy with juice, the sweet pulp warmed
    and waiting for your mouth. I would offer you some
    from my hand, the largest of the acreage,

but I don't know where you are. If they find me here
    —drifter, derelict—I will not resist;
    their sudden knives will find an easy home
    in this body I've always known

I'd have to return. Mind, too, will be given back—
    its familiar wanderings, its always-running scripts,
    filmic sweeps, delusional digressions
    and unapologetic codes—all reclaimed.

The prized, nearly infinite catalog of memories—
    you float toward aspen branches on the swing,
    it must be July and nearing
    four dozen years, that much light;

you heave Father's maul against all of winter
    into the snowman with the plaid scarf,
    the day he left you, that much gravity;
    you bury the blue parakeet in a perfume box

beneath the clematis that smothers the white rail fence;
    the bright smut in his drawer
    under his socks and one silk tie;
    young tongues touch in a movie theater,

so much ignorance to undo;
    night car tailed by the moon—
    the whole cavalcade of your personal history,
    its crush, its pursuing phantoms—

November apples, Grandmother throwing herself on his coffin,
    the single white rose, bluegill thrashing in a net,
    that much purpose; sister's painful braces,
    your cousin's breasts, that much want;

your pencil ticks across the page, the empowerment
    of the first undetected lie, the first
    gray hair, the first and the last
    comingling—all of these reclaimed.

I pour the wine into the crock to season the pork.
    You will continue for now, the steaming stew says.
    And the placid, fast-moving clouds—
    as if dragged above a stage on pulleys and invisible wire,

their ample bulk infused with varicolored light—ask,
    Do you think you've been sent here
    without purpose? The audience not allowing
    themselves to awaken

from the fictive dream. *Here, here,* the star is calling to us,
    her hands holding forth something,
    impressing us to take—round, dark
    grapes. *I've brought these for you. They braved me*

with their knives, and now I know. Eat, she implores,
    her forty-something years of training condensed
    into this one urgency,
    our hundreds of eyes upon her, but none of us moving,

none reaching, all frightened slightly, all certain
    that we need only to maintain our impassive roles,
    to follow the script we believe
    has, thus far, excluded us.

2

A violent revocation rehearsed by many at midlife: the hard-
    won but now paltry trophies
    revoked, the taken-for-granted, well-oiled
    charms revoked, the wetted

loins revoked, one's value, one's place, one's solipsistic
    certainties asunder or slipping
    or gone. I look at my hands
    from what suddenly seems fifty feet away,

emblems of panic. Which messengers are we to trust?
    From the master builder's rejected stones
    one will be selected—
    years later, reclaimed

from the thistle patch—to be employed as the keystone.
    I recognize the mirror's face and the self associated
    with it, but the relationship
    between them is

rent, map that no longer matches the terrain.
    A voice—mine?—*Here is the perfection*
    you have elsewhere sought. I'm steering
    the organism I've mistaken as me

through the blackened thistles, compelled,
    like them, by the need for light.

3

Seeking beauty amidst silent turmoil,
 predictably, I courted a woman half my age.
 The obvious discrepancies between us
 brought no shame

but were inflamed reminders of being alive
 in a tempest of interiority.
 Three years previous, she'd been violently raped;
 initially, attempting to have sex

would make her run retching to the toilet, but with time
 I could enter her and hold her eyes,
 and with further time she relearned
 how to come, and her menstruation,

which had ceased, returned, a kind of thaw.
 I say this not to justify what many
 would consider my transgression
 but to report facts that were mysterious to us.

Now I find myself again in the vineyard. I have a wife
 and a nursing child. I've built a tower
 and I watch over the countryside
 which is mine,

which is irrigated and bountiful, which yields riches
 that I turn into feast and finery. One evening
 men arrive bearing official documents
 proclaiming the land I have worked is not mine.

We argue. I send them away but give them replenishments
 of water, fruit, and bread
 poisoned with aconite.
 Tomorrow I will find them dead

and push them into the ravine and burn their scrolls
    and watch the wax seals pool
    then bubble and blacken.

4

I've arrived at the rich man's vineyard. My documents are in order.
    Tomorrow I will announce his eviction.
    Overcome by the beauty of the glowing
    hillside, I ask my frequent question,

How can we ever repay you, God? And I am struck
    by the first stone, implausible
    as thunder from blue sky.
    I won't remember falling or the rough voices

of the men who strangle my throat with plaited rope
    or in which direction I am dragged or how
    my body—the vessel, the leased vehicle—
    tumbles into a ravine, spilling its elixirs

that have kept me alive, kept me here, in a place I always thought
    separate from You.
    Then I am an inexplicable kind of self
    before a face I've never seen yet somehow remember,

a face smiling, in perpetuity and beyond corruption.

HART & SWORD

(Psalm 42)

We set the clocks back an hour so when dawn comes I am awake.
    I dreamed of being chased again—sometimes a car,
    sometimes a carriage. I tell you this while still coming to,
    some part or place of me panting, having run so far:
    the hunted hart thirsting for water,

a metaphor for the neglected soul, but speaking of it fails it—
    the folly of a language that demands objects
    must have a possessor: *my* soul, as if the inverse isn't
    more true: the feeble *I* but a dream within the soul's
    vaster cognition. November dawn, southerly sun,

the first wicked lace of frost on windowpanes.
    We hung the birdfeeder too close to the bush and now
    have to baffle the squirrels with a metal hood
    too wide to circumvent. Maybe this will serve as a metaphor
    for the relationship between mind and soul:

cardinal inside the burning bush, vermillion inside vermillion:
    temporary shelter, contentment, containment, camouflage,
    ruse, agent and agency. I woke knowing the dream
    from which I'd come had presence but not locus. I write,
    "Being *here* or *there* is a condition unique

to embodiment." Here I am; there you are, my love: an inconvenient—
    but delicious—economy. Tea kettle, feed the cat, commute,
    corn fields cut to stubble. I write: "In every village
    there is a tabernacle, but each time I step inside,
    there is no tabernacle"—trying again to convince myself

that holiness is not an external enterprise, an idea that justifies
    my lack of participation in a faith. Etymologically, tabernacle is
    the tent of the seer. Today, where do we go to see
    what we need to see? And would we dare see it?
    And why does this example come to mind?

At night, when they shower, the college students don't
　　close their blinds, and I go through the contortions
　　of noticing but not allowing myself to look. Poor eyes, so many
　　masters to serve—body, mind, and soul. And which wants
　　to see, which turns away? The ancients say the tears we cry

are the soul's meat, but the soul cannot feast, for only mouthèd
　　is the body. I write: "Mind and soul and body are the three
　　cords of a braid." Like your braids, which I touch now
　　while you sleep, the little tremors of a dream
　　playing in your fingers and face. My hart,

what hunts us? Is asking for soul asking for God?
　　The forest burns, and upon the pursuing riders' swords
　　is etched "The Abyss calls forth the Abyss." I wake, I write:
　　"We emerge from *wherelessness* and to *wherelessness*
　　we go." The snow has come. In high limbs, crows,

winter crows, which are also summer crows, cawing, crying,
　　and—I'm convinced—rejoicing.

PACIFIC CLIFFS

this used to be the edge of the world

an horizon to elicit the hope and bewilderment

that some initial desire created us

a love replete with boundaries

and the means to transgress them

the awful mystery of a boat

before there ever was a sea

grant me that possibility

I, like you, am still being made

A QUESTION

I've asked this question many times it knows me
I've run from it kneeled for it burned it it is me

we've come we've cried we've kept most of our secrets
for centuries for seasons for seconds we've been breathing

to enact Your dreams Your dramas Your dances
to orbit before the obituary the eye of the lover

to have him to have her to be had and had again
without limit my lecher my liege my sanctified receiver

what will you call me when my calling goes quiet
my dark then light my darker commander

TO A FUTURE SELF

because you will think
that *the way* is through the heart

because unwittingly
you will seek an exit through the senses

because they won't teach you to laugh
you will preserve it when you can

joy's petite spasm in a notebook
and call it *mine*

because you will ask
why this incarceration in a body

to become to feel to fail to flower

the tide will come at the chartable hour
late spring clouds taller

much taller than cities than mountains
taller than all the empires' ambitions

and made of vapor

LOVE SONG FOR THE NEW WORLD

(Catedral de Sevilla)

1

In the altar of La Virgen del Madroño, Mary offers her gilt breast.
    What else could a woman do in 1454? Give suck or burn
    with the faggots. The origin of the derogatory metaphor:
    lynched, murdered, beaten into comas, boys who looked wrongly
    at, say, the muscled reapers or

men who, despite caution, were discovered together in barns
    and groves—these thrown down *like bundles of sticks* to be
    part of the fire, the spectacle, the offering to the unnamed
    place in us we've made whole religions to displace.
    But the Child refuses her milk

and refuses what the kneeling angel offers, the sweet fruits of the World,
    turning instead to look at me, His center, with eyes of wood,
    until I'm stolen by the seven circling swallows in this
    space vast enough to hold other cathedrals entire, their swift
    sickle bodies not frantic, not

looking to land—who knows if it's joy or panic that fuels them—
    and only rarely tricked or enticed to try the false sky
    that entranced Saint Anthony for four hundred years,
    the bright white vortex churning with cherubim. Actually
    the bewitched saint had a few weeks

reprieve from the terrific light of God: sliced from the larger whole,
    he stole to New York before being discovered and returned
    and stitched nearly invisibly back into place, having learned
    the futility of escape. Poor Anthony, saint of amputees and
    barrenness, dying under the walnut tree

at thirty-five, poisoned slowly by obscure fungus, vomiting, rotting
    at the ends of his limbs, edematous and desquamated, saint of
    shipwrecks and runts of litters, seizing and seeing nonetheless
    the beauty within a child and weeping, his hands curled like
    the knots of nautical ropes—saint of

lost articles—given over to an invisible fire that would be named
    for him. They lovingly cut out his tongue and vocal cords for
    the Holy Reliquary where they were implored long after
    becoming black dust. I'm sorry. I lost myself. It is in here
    too large, but who isn't—unto some force

we cannot answer because we cannot know—lost? "Moreno de verde
    luna," *dark of the green moon*, Federico García Lorca wrote,
    when the stars nail spears on the grey water, murdered
    on a road outside Granada, night anonymous, *there were four*
    daggers and he could only succumb,

faggot for the knives again, faggot of no body. When they exhumed him
    he was not there, my little vanished Jesus, may you be—
    if you can still be—laughing and fucking as we go on
    inside a balloon of blood we mistake for a sky. In my absence,
    the brown widows have taken over

2

my barn, but what need do I have for a barn? Their egg sacs like lost
    ornaments for The Virgin gathered and repurposed here.
    Maybe I'll vacuum them all away. I don't know, I'm sick
    of the killings. Can't we just watch the ten boys dance,
    three times a year, in their unblemished

white and light blue to mark our memories, their bodies unsexed,
    hats with plumes, tasseled castanets, to mark us with
    (*inmaculada concepción*) how unmarked she was, white slippers,
white belts, white knickers where their nuts are held, un-
    dropped, unhaired, unable yet to make

any other world, dressed as the pages of Philip III, pages of celebration
  —what might a white page become? These bloodless words
  I've given myself to, in my way, trying to make meaning
  if not art, leading me, sometimes, to understanding and
  sometimes to a request for forgiveness

but of what I don't know or don't verbalize: the Seed in the fertile
  ground put there by what hand, what rod? Without guilt
  Mary offers her breast and the metaphor opens its mouth,
  toothless, for now. My shirt was made in Honduras.
  I'm a little ashamed

3

of everything I own. Saint Francis in his Apotheosis is carried skyward
  by a host of winged children. He wears a gown given to him by
  Mary, woven by angels, the story goes, and without a seam,
  a perfect envelope for his perfect renunciation. I'm the man in
  the foreground, fallen back from the sight,

gravity bound and full of flaws, arm raised ambiguously to shield
  or embrace, the nearest floating boy, peenie small as a
  fingertip, gleefully holding aloft a human skull. The simple
  persistent fable: be good enough and you'll ascend. So faithful,
  so sympathetic that he bled where

Jesus had bled, the first stigmatic, father of a new kind of blood.
  Did you hear that Manuel Antonio Rodolfo Quinn Oaxaca when playing
  the Hunchback of Notre Dame was so "in character" that
  he grew carbuncles? I love the scene where she gives him water
  and the kindness is more than he can bear,

but he responds by yelling "thank you" like a monster. There are
        better versions. As children, my brother had a repertoire
        of Quasimodo imitations. In my favorite, he would hobble
        to his knees, face twisted, and nearly weeping whisper in bliss,
        slobber froth forming around his mouth,

"She gave me water." The gift from the perfect one. To drink from
        that which is pure. The cup of blood becomes a chalice of
        water. But dangerous to covet that which is pure—Lorca's Rosa
        de los Cambrios, whose tits were sliced off and presented on
        a plate. "Black are the horses . . .

and they hide in their skulls / a vague astronomy / of shapeless pistols."
        I bought this shirt because it was perfect for my needs,
        a lapel I'll never iron, a fabric that holds the shape
        I'm destined to give away. In a robe of cobalt Saul has fallen
        beneath the stained-glass sky

4

and no one but him knows why. He wears a helmet of war, for the road
        to Damascus was to end with captives. The Son of Man said,
        "I will show him how much he must suffer for my name." Then
        a sight-stealing flash. Pained, the white horse rolls beneath him,
        in the mindless dust the red sash

of the Office. When after three days Ananais removes the curse with his
        magical hands, the blindness falls from his eyes like scales.
        Ergo: even the most wicked can be transformed by God's love,
        and even the most loved will be punished. Reject or accept
        the calculus, this window has narrated

the story for five hundred years. The oldest trees in Iowa were alive
    during the Civil War. No vertebrate lives longer than
    the Greenland shark, four hundred years, reaching sexual
    maturity at one-fifty. Look up. The light comes through
    this story and into your eyes. How much

does it matter what you believe? Saul—Paul—he was both and neither.
    Our words are mummy cloth, giving shape to what is gone.
    If you were to enter from the courtyard, you would walk through
    the Door of Forgiveness. It's easy to want it from others.
    Put away your camera and brochures,

5

kneel here on your suntanned knees, eyes closed against
    a light that's grown impossible to ignore, the single searing
    flame of your regrets—voice them now—and then crawl
    through. I'll be on the other side with my selfie-stick
    asking WTF? My own mistake

having already delivered me, immigrant of accident, to maplessness,
    queasy from eating again the same words, mantra of misfortune
    tattooed inside my throat—"my"?—*this* throat I've been loaned.
    But there are thousands we can join who've come to see her,
    the Virgin of the Kings, who has listened,

in her way, for eight hundred years to the whispers of hope and grief.
    Her golden head fitted with a mechanism that allows someone
    out of view to turn her eyes so that you are beheld as you
    come and go. Why not make material our needs? Some deacon
    perhaps in 1285 puppeteering

the Mother of God, with the intensity of one who not only believes but
     whose career depends upon the verity of a look. Blessed Mother,
     Star of the Sea, Most Holy, Most Pure, did you ask for the burden
     of authority? Outside the late light is in the orange trees and on
     the tile worn concave by the friction

of feet. Scaffolding is up but the workers have gone home. Pigeons
     found one lamppost without plastic spikes, and a woman,
     pointing, describes to a child in a language—maybe Dutch—
     something I do not see. And then it comes back, my old disgust
     for these icons—the pious, upward

6

gazes, the nearly naked, nonsexual bodies, idealized and static,
     the dusty narrative of grace. Try to think of them, the anonymous
     guilds of fathers and sons every day—for lifetimes—beside the
     scorching ovens, glazing tiles for a pittance, and the neophytes
     of Zurbarán's school, some anxious,

some euphoric, mixing the pigments of the Master. Did they sketch
     each other in private, tongues out, eyes crossed in fun, or
     cocks in hand, in postures grotesque, ass to sky? And what
     became of her, the young woman I dreamt up, who wrapped
     her breasts tight beneath her smocks

and brushed her checks with charcoal dust to appear an unshaven man?
     When she was discovered and the circle closed around her and
     the robes were cast aside, which master intervened, which watched?
     In her open book Saint Theresa puts the words, read by
     the black sockets of a skull

and flown toward by the white spirit dove, the unfailing arrow. Shoeless,
if they were allowed to show her feet. In tears, intoxicated in
body, memory, and imagination by God, if it were possible
to depict. Absolved of the Inquisition. We understand you even
less today than then, but

7

thank you, and here are two flowers, wild indigo and blue rattlesnake
master to stick in the eyeholes. May someone paint them in.
In the village of Medinaceli in the region of Castilla y León,
each November a bull is fixed with a wooden collar and false
horns coated in tar and turpentine

that protrude above its own. Then tied to posts and held by the bravest
men, torches touch the armature till alight. Toro de Fuego.
Loosed among the people who fill the plaza, aflame, afraid,
goaded. Toro de Jubilo, two thousand years older than
(*septem digitorum*) the crucifying

nails, the shroud of blood, the cup of blood. Two and a half millennia
older than these cathedral walls I've stepped outside of
into another ostensibly perfect day. Which leads me to belief,
the false blossom of it, the promise of arrival in a story
that can have no end.

In the twenty-first century the bull does not die, but its ears might melt,
dripping like candles. And make no mistake, the bull is
revered, paradoxically, in the destruction of what it symbolizes:
strength, virility, bounty—what we wish to know or become.
When the Nazarene was lowered

from the cross-timbers, he was already nearly entirely an idea.
    Pietà: piety: dutifulness. In Francisco Bayeu's version
    of the trope, the sky she gazes into is an impenetrable umber.
    For thousands of years the bull is bled and butchered and fed
    to us, the people of the village,

who dance. An umber darker than night because spot-lit are mother
    and son alone in the searing light of consequence. Before
    and after unimaginably charged. Not haloed, she nor he.
    The hoop of thorns on the ground, still worthless; it was never
    a crown despite his torturers'

belief in irony: a symbol requires subscription to be imbued
    with power. When the bull thunders through the citizens
    wearing its halo of fire, in the Plaza Mayor, circled by the five
    fires of the Holy Martyrs, those who remain still are unharmed,
    if the bull's belief in stillness

remains. *The Descent* by Pedro de Campaña has Christ's face shadowed
    by the large body and cloaks of a man on a ladder helping
    to lift him down. Partially occluded the face is less face than
    skull, hence the symbol is made material—the act *is* death
    and geography: *Gulgulta*, place

of the skull. And Martâ, saint, witness of magic and resurrection, why,
    nearly hidden in your hair and gown, mistaken almost for
    an exposed breast—why do you bear a human skull? Hand on
    the cross, pained in expression, a spark radiating from what once
    was your fontanelle, where, before

the bone-gate of innocence shut, a luminous string, dangerously thin,
    still tethered you to God, now a phosphorous white spark—why
    the mind case of what is no more? We need not ask, really.
    The jubilation would not be complete without beef stew.
    Thick chunks of meat nearly too

8

big to bite, perfect after a touch of salt. What more is required of us
   than to *incorporate* the sacrifice? In the Sacristy of Chalices,
   Francisco Goya's saints, Justa and Rufina, out of place, calm
   from the singularity of their attention to the divine
   without and within, and the starving

lions captured, caged and cargoed thousands of miles (land and sea)
   for this one purpose: to eat, in front of all, these women whose
   piety offends and whose devotion enrages. But the lions,
   heavier than three men and stronger than ten, cower
   and come forth crawling, awkwardly,

against the impeccable gracefulness and feral disobedience of their kind,
   to lick the women's naked feet. How the hundreds watching
   low, initially, in disappointment, and laugh, and then,
   struck aware by a solemn gravity, are silent. How the keeper
   of lions, bearing a trident and whip,

goes forth to prod and yell, but when his eyes touch the somehow joyful
   face of Santa Rufina, he kneels and begins to sob. How the gasps
   and murmurs of the crowd send a current of fear then disbelief
   then fury through the prefect himself, how his scrotum contracts
   in his woolen robes, how

one nod to his general sends him and entourage, pugios drawn,
   to the slaughter-circus floor. Pitiful how the beheading blade
   lodges between the cervical vertebrae, how the strong squirt
   squirt squirt of blood from the still-pumping heart
   paints his polished cuirass.

The magnificent shame that pierces all watchers then, as if
   a dart shot by the sniper's art. Look deeply, Goya insisted.
   Broken, in the dirt, a regal statue head. Painter of the Court,
   artist of the State, he goes deaf, he goes into isolation,
   he saw the world undone and

survived. Renouncing notoriety he paints his final works on the plaster
     walls of his home, the *Pinturas Negras*: a lone dog on a dune,
     two men beating each other bloody with cudgels, a goat-headed
     orator, old naked and bulging-eyed a god eats his tiny son,
     women, if you can call them that,

9

laughing. Kneel with me at the Altar de Plata. Above us shine
     the eighty-five spikes of the glowing silver sun,
     sun within sun, warmth and light radiating outward,
     making another of itself, sun within a son. Restored
     after Napoleon's thugs melted it

two hundred years ago to finance their war. *Deum de Deo*. Brazen,
     the phalanx of boots on the tile echo. Sanctity or saber,
     Master or musket? *Lumen de lúmine*. Kneel with me
     in the aftershock of history, at the little ancient fence
     that keeps us from touching

the symbols we've come thousands of miles to know. Kneel with me
     beneath the crown unwearable, the candles unlit, surveillance
     cameras and dustless shepherds' crooks. Kneel with me
     and bring it forth from inside you—from all that is seen and
     unseen—the silence.

Two and a half years—a wink, an eternity—the army could not be
     repelled, resistance sentiment strong but unable to organize.
     Kneel with me in the cradling arms of history,
     in the quiet that follows stampedes. Sunlight clocks
     its brilliance around the halo

of spikes. How many hundreds of silver flowers—thicker only slightly
than the actual, forged of molten earth yet breakable with one
squeeze—adorn us? I dreamt of them again, the 15th-century nuns
who laid illegitimate orphans in cradles lined with spikes
and rocked them until

10

the stone-vaulted corridors were silent. Because heaven is more
receptive of souls who have suffered. Stained glass of
a beheaded saint—sapphire blue, cousin's rose, yellow
of crushed mustard. I wake to what I am
so sure of—and this is how

each day begins in error. For seven centuries they have called it
"cathedral lizard," the wooden crocodile suspended above
the Courtyard of Oranges, a facsimile of the living original
that was offered as a gift by an Egyptian emir to King Alfonzo X
when asking for his daughter's hand.

O Andalusia. O royal offspring, skin the color of tea with milk.
He who wasn't born, wasn't conceived, except in numerous
imaginations. The gifts to trade for her exotic, regal body
and prestige: one tusk of ivory, one baton (symbol of justice),
one crocodile, and one giraffe, neither

of which lived long, such is the nature of exile. Intricate channels
irrigate the citrus in a patio entirely stone. When they bloom
in concert, if your heart is open and your mind singular,
there is no wish that cannot become. The emir also offered
a bridle for reasons unclear—

apparently it was the wrong time of year. I breathe deeply, deeply until
I can hold no more, my face in the waxy green leaves, imagining
the white and small spring blooms, symmetry parted to reveal
the universe's center exposed ten thousand times in this
single square, imagining

the illegitimate son delivered and barely wiped of womb blood, one
hour before the cock, by a nurse veiled and rushed, to be sung to
in the chamber of merciful cradles, imagine him secreted instead
to a faithful baker's wife then to a tinker, who in dawn light
on donkeyback to a rowboat goes,

committing his life's only transgression, imagining him grown and
gowned in white and fanning himself in the rare humidity
of summer rain, Moroccan tea and biscuits of almond and
anise, having returned, young, newly bearded man,
to the land of his birth,

11

scrotum so full of worlds that it would be a falsehood not to be a king.
In Ramón Bayeu's painting of San Sebastián, they are almost
invisible in the naked young man's muscular abdomen and
upper thigh: two arrows. Historical accounts say that when
Roman archers tied him

to a post and practiced their aim, he was more full of pricks
than a hedgehog. Again the divine spotlight, again the flushed
face upturned, more than half gone already to a passion
beyond pain, the bound wrists holding up and back the arms,
exposing fully the nearly

translucent pectorals that could hold you strongly—how many
thousands of men have wished this throughout time?—
but offer no shield to shaft-shuttled tip. Saint of the plague.
Saint of closet cases, earner of God's protection. Once, that is,
not twice. When from the wounds

he did not die, he sought Diocletian, yet another emperor of Christian
nightmares, and publicly harangued him. Fists and clubs,
shattered bones, hemorrhaging organs. Tossed pulpy
in the sewer. The upturned top of his skull was silver cast
and used as a drinking cup by

devotees seven hundred years later. So persuasive was he that his
earliest captors would release him from incarceration,
they now Christians too. He a soldier himself, a captain
of Praetorian guards, hiding among his enemies, but
he didn't regard them as such.

Not party, not nationality, not affiliation—the real enemies are
your thoughts, each its own wind, pushing your boat,
gust by gust to where, perhaps unwittingly, you command it.
Just two arrows, Bayeu decided. Maybe that's the real story.
A Lazian field in February,

a relentless wind bearing a chill from Lapland tundra. Disinterested
or disagreeing, *thwock thwock* go the bowstrings, two weak
shots aimed low. And when the man cries out, a cry so
animal and pathetic, a single syllable wordless howl
that is the sound of empire,

a second-rank centurion history never cared to remember says,
Enough. And as he turns to walk away, beads of mizzle
run from his red wool cape. Her tears are carved of wood
and she keeps vigil in the Chapel of Sorrows. Shellacked
or glazed, it takes little imagination

12

for her cheeks to be wet from an unending grief. In some depictions
    her pierced heart is the hub of a wheel of daggers. Lucent,
    pure—one cheek pale, one rouged. Local lore says a drunk
    Protestant smashed her face with a wine bottle, but the only
    effect was that she became more

lifelike. Asymmetrical, five emerald brooches bloom at her breast,
    pinned there by Joselito Gómez Ortega of bullfighting's
    golden age. For him—and him alone in history—she wore
    black at his early death. My camera drifts over her bodice,
    zooms in, clarifies this eye,

so perfect and so limited: only the outward signs of the holy grief
    do I capture. Bless us, Jacob (Ya'akov, Yaaqob-el), as you did
    your many sons, that we, too, may live 147 years. Perhaps
    then we will weep them as well, tears without end. Israel—
    namesake and father of an entire

faith—immigrant welcomed into Egypt when drought cast you
    and yours away, how have we gone astray? I saw them
    on the television in the airport, hungry, in the tent city,
    fenced, patrolled, those who've fled worse than famine.
    Wooden tears. Wooden tears

for all sixty million of them and their alien needs: warmth, drink,
    a night for dreams. Thick, sumptuous, crimson
    cloth covers the walls of the Chapterhouse, handwoven
    but machine-precise, a tower flanked by lilies—no flaw,
    no interruption in the pattern,

13

no escape—it will outlive us. Would you expect less of empire?
 One table, one wooden throne from 1592 from which
 you are faced by no less than all of history, its cavernous
 ceiling, Doric entablature, geometric skylights (two windows
 per season), stoic kings, pedigreed

patrons, thirteen-foot Virgin, the only being ever completely un-
 fucked by anything, even God, the fecund center at the
 center of the room, in the center of the cathedral, in the
 center of the city, in the center of the kingdom that is the
 center of the civilization

central in the centrifuge that is God's heart, which is the absolute
 ideation of Center, the placelessness from which place is
 possible. The throne is empty. We're on vacation.
 The tour group is two rooms away. Have a seat.
 I'll watch the door. Go ahead.

14

Have a seat and from all of there, ask. . . . Help me. Help me remedy
 the irony that baby Jesus is made of gold and silver
 extracted—one speck or less per pail—from earth's insides
 by slaves weak from alien sicknesses, curse-
 breeze in their mouths.

Baby Jesus, so pure and emblematic. How not even records
 were kept of their numbers, let alone who they might have been
 in the fields of the Lord before the Lord's people arrived.
 (Irony seeds irony.) Buried here, Colón, the son of Colombo,
 another man who changed this

world that can only change. Used his father's wealth to build
an unparalleled library, patron of bookmakers, keeper of
incunabula. In a vellum poster from his collection, a white
snake wiggles from the mouth and eye hole of a skull—
remember when the class clown

threaded a spaghetti noodle through his nose and out his mouth then
"flossed" it back and forth?—the skeleton's clavicles
anatomically incorrect, more like scapular armor than
the most fragile of the body's large bones. Two more skulls,
one with a bludgeon wound, gaze

at the inscrutable text at the center, tablets in the hands of Moses,
mistakenly horned—so affected by divine encounter—
and the red sleeves of his gown bloom outward, an opulent,
shiny vulva that the nearly toothless skull leans to taste.
Allegory of the Transience.

15

I'm avoiding telling you about him, Christoforo, intimidated by
how much there is to say. He's buried here, most believe;
though it was disputed as recently as 2006. His bones
and guts-gone-to-dust moved five times, back and forth
from worlds old and new.

But you know the story, the one that begins in elementary
school with the names of three ships and doesn't ever end?
More people at this tomb than the crosses of Christ, more
here than the three-story altar of gold so delicate and thin
it could be worn. How stern

the faces of the casket carriers, how imperturbable in monumental
    scale. The castle, the lion, bipedal and crowned, the cape
    of bats, insignia that traps the eye. The more symbolically
    imbued, the greater the cultural value. Tassel of bells,
    tassel of shells, tassel at the throat

and heart. Five feathers from five eagles, black and gold the wings
    enfold, and the words frame us all. Fence of poppies.
    The oar, the Asiatic fish, gauntlet of Genoan leather.
    Small windows, no glass, repeated along the castle walls
    in the shape of—what else?—

the cross. Slender opening, half the width of a man, from which
    the surroundings can be surveyed and defended
    with arrows, stones, and boiling water. Black cross
    in white wall; cross of light in black wall: the murder hole.
    Armor-piercing crossbow bolt

fletched by feathers of the dove. I, Christopher, share his name.
    Cristóbal. "Bearer of Christ—*Portador de Cristo*." From
    the Greek, *the anointed*, the selected, the one rubbed
    with the oil. Unguent, the successor. *Mashah*, the messiah.
    A pomegranate offered

16

on the blade of a lance. He wanted to help them. Ten times
    to the new world and ten times back, Bartolomé de la Casas,
    black robe, counselor for a future he would never see,
    on the beguiling shore of Hispaniola, saw them roped
    and naked and bash-brained

and gashed and knew that something other than this was
   the right way. He watched when many had to turn away,
   thirteen at a time suspended alive from the gibbets, their feet
   allowed to barely touch the ground—thirteen: the Redeemer
   and his twelve—then lit

by a slow fire from below. So awful were the howls that the captain
   required the next thirteen first be gagged. "The Lord is
   only for them," he would chant when sleep wouldn't come,
   "that wait upon him in the way of truth and justice."
   When a consort of a Taíno chief

was abducted and raped, the outnumbered Spaniards were set upon,
   but the clubs of reeds were little more than boys' playthings,
   and the bodies of the Taíno soon became practice for sword
   and spear. Most points were earned when a torso could be
   cleaved in one fierce slash.

"To whom doth he look, and who in his strength?" The light suggests
   siesta. Even the cathedral quiet is quieter. *Forgive us.*
   The hour to shutter the shops, to twist closed the blinds, to
   forestall the longer sleep with the shorter, to bring him
   to you in this cheated hour,

to undo the apron strings, to shut the laptop, to rest in the scent
   of her hair, to share the pillow. *Magua, forgive us.* To sit
   on the ancient pew, the hard-assed pew, and be here. *Forgive
   us, Marien. Forgive us, Maquana, Xaraqua, and Hiquey.*
   "In Three or Four Months time

I being there present, Six Thousand Children and upward were
   murder'd because they had lost their Parents who labour'd
   in the Mines; nay I was a Witness of many other stupendous
   Villanies." No, don't forgive. I chant it in the wee temple
   at the center of my heart:

17

don't forgive don't forgive don't—an endless cretic meter: wave and
    shore, cloud and void, shave and war. The stone pillows
    that hold the stone head of Cardinal Juan de Cervantes
    is exemplary sculptural realism. The sheen of rock may as well
    be the sheen of silk,

and notice how the pillows crater in the center and puff outward,
    as if half made of air, not solid alabaster. I like the small
    deer curled at his dead feet, content as a domesticated dog.
    He's been inside the sarcophagus 564 years. That means
    he's been nothing but bones

for half a millennium, the tissue taking fifty years to fully rot away
    when thus entombed. He's flanked by angels—and why not?
    He's flanked by wise men in robes and lions and—why not?—
    more deer and four rising or setting suns and interposing
    crosses and an intricate background

of white bells that can't ring. I like that such effort went into making
    his face and hands and pillows look wholly veritable,
    while gravity does little to the gowns that wrap him,
    as if he's floating not lying—weight being something
    we also will surrender.

18

I'm about to let you go. I'm leaving; you're leaving too. Every
    apparently infrangible being is leaving. There will be
    a parade in the streets when we go. So bright the light
    we will feel assaulted by warmth and the vision demanded
    of us, a taxation of the eyes

without end. But it will be a quiet parade, soft, piano music beyond
two walls, and children will lead it, but don't mistake that
for symbolism; their hatred is as pure as glacier and as white.
The Nazarenes of the Confraternity of Silence will have the street.
Tailored and shining, their gowns,

cummerbunds, and colorful cords. Staff of red oak, cross of silver. Three feet
will rise their pointed caps, unflagging, erect, sharp as
ibis beaks. White satin, purple velour. Their hands will be
gloved, faces veiled, opaque, and only their eyes, from perfect
holes the size of quarter dollars,

will betray their humanness. *Semana Santa*. Black cloak and drum.
Cape of teal, crimson veil, golden chevron. White drape,
red cross at heart, cross in circle, red circle, blood, wine,
bond, law. The precise trajectory is lost—how this ancient
sect became inspiration for more

wickedness in the new world. "KKK" autocorrected to "kill."
How anonymity catalyzes hate. A teacher, tired at the end
of a school day, I sit in a student desk and watch
a wind-tangled shopping bag shred in a sapling's twigs.
Carved beside my hand

in the hard plastic, crude small cuts, a swastika, the size of a fingernail.
I find a scrap of sandpaper and try to work it away, but
the friction blemishes the surface and only darkens the etch,
making it more visible. What season is it? And a poem—
shouldn't it do more at the end?

A field, perhaps, at the edge of a town somewhere in the Midwest.
The brassy, long hours of summer. Wild yarrow, profligate,
white and filigreed as lace, acrawl with hoverflies, lighter
than the blooms which bend and loll in an erratic wind,
and the flies ride them seemingly without effort as they eat.

BLOOD ARIA

How do I use my bulletproof backpack?

Hold the bag between yourself and the threat using the straps as handles. Use it as a shield to provide cover for your upper torso (vital organs).

—FREQUENTLY ASKED QUESTIONS, BULLET BLOCKER®

And the Lord said unto Cain, Where is Abel thy brother? And he said, I know not: Am I my brother's keeper?

—GENESIS 4:9

So the story goes, the first human born
is a murderer—*morð*, secret killing. And when Earth
drinks the blood, the Lord hears screaming.

Despite three thousand teenagers inside,
what the first-responders hear is silence.
When the rounds hit hit hit hit hit

a body, they fragment, four bullets in one:
goodbye lung, goodbye liver, heart, bladder—
house of the soul in the Inuit myth, where raven

pierces the first bladder to let out light, hence day;
then Father takes it away, hence night. In the documentary
the paramedic says that when the first body

was carried from the school toward the ambulance,
she was relieved, knowing she could help, could
make something right. But then she saw

what had become of the six-year-old, barely
held together anymore. There is a pause, long for television—
five years after the massacre, she still can't

tell the story. My mind fills in the details: like a marionette
whose strings are cut. It's never answered why God was
impressed by the firstling of the flock but not

the fruit of the field. The favor of the Father,
the first source of envy. Such a male story: emphasis on
act and consequence, duty before dignity,

feelings that touch bathos then retreat into
minutiae. In the livestream of the rampage, the surprising
loudness of the shots makes end-users on every continent

flinch. What once was a girl is lifted—blood puddle,
bright tile. Cain excited or terrified by the color inside
Edenic kin? They always say it:

We never thought it would happen here. I said it too.
Tucson, Arizona; October 29, 2002. For five days news vans
are parked along the streets. I walk past before they go live,

the reporter checks his hair in the reflection of the window.
Cathy pops into my office: *Lock your door, there's a shooter
in the building.* I wasn't afraid until

I peeked into the hall, saw a black-clad SWAT team
scooting along the wall, rifles held vertical, a strict formality
that made the whole world seem shabby. It wasn't real

until then, and then nothing was real. *Let us go into the field,*
the first brother says. The killer writes a twenty-page letter
detailing how he's been wronged. Religious scholars justify

God's bias, noting that Abel gave the best of his flock,
but nowhere in the canon does it say that Cain
gave the best of his field. The professor crawls beneath

the desk and begs to remain alive. Inside of time.
Bound by identity. Bound by body. Nourished by the un-
believably red rivers that comprise us, that flow and pulse

and carry, please, more oxygen, *Please, I have a daughter.*
Her name is Sam. In one version of the story, Eve is raped
by an archon, but we reject this for it offers a way out;

the mythic fundament is that inside each of us
is Cain. The dude on Facebook I haven't seen since high school
said the government's coming for all the guns.

If only God was in people's homes, he waxes,
this would never happen. And then it happens again.
I am driving, the radio says forty-nine dead.

It happens again. I'm at a party and the news interrupts
and the music responds *Turn off the hope you had for me,*
Turn on the voice that cries again. I am walking and see

a helicopter circling and I know it's happening—
Turn off the lights, turn on the rain. The older brother
puts his hand on the small of the younger's back

and leads him to the ultimate unnamed thing.
During the funeral service we release three white doves.
We had to obtain a special permit from the County.

Had we been unable, our backup plan was balloons,
until someone said, This is not a *celebration*—the word
drawn out as the tears turned on and our faces became

masks of Greek tragedy. Some of us still go around that way,
unable to right the frown. It's been seventeen years.
The corners of our eyes reaching down

almost to the jawline. *Can you hear them?* I'm asked
in a dream as I pick up the shining casings.
And for a moment I do, like a sudden

soundtrack, screams of joy and laughter in the empty
playground. Each day I think—fifteen, twenty, fifty times—
if the shooting begins now, what will I do?

In the bathroom, copy room, lunchroom, parking lot?
In the library with the twelve-year-olds
in their favorite shirts and bangles, rounding the hall corner

hit hit hit as the smoke bombs ignite? In the documentary
the janitor asks rhetorically *Does a day go by*
when I don't think of it? Abel turns, surprised.

Does an hour go by? One white dove flies, lands in a tree
and stays until we begin to fold up the chairs. *Do five minutes*
go by without thinking of it? Cain, aching

for Father-love, lifts a spike like a raven's beak.
It can't always be light, the first story reminds.
And when the world breaks, you look for yourself
                                        in the details.

WINTERSEED

what could have been
still shining
in the broken
bast and baddened blooms
what might yet be
abides
with little room and no conception
of hope worthless
and practically invisible
you are
already found

ACKNOWLEDGMENTS

I am grateful to the Jacob K. Javits Fellowship Program and the Dorothy Sargent Rosenberg Memorial Fund for support that helped make this book possible. Many of these poems first appeared in two chapbooks, *Capital City at Midnight*, which was awarded the 2014 *BLOOM* Prize, and *Love Song for the New World*, published in 2019 in the Editor's Series of Seven Kitchens Press. For being champions of this book in its various stages, I offer my gratitude to Sean Bishop, Gabrielle Calvocoressi, Charles Flowers, Jane Miller, Ron Mohring, Boyer Rickel, Natasha Trethewey, and Ronald Wallace. Fond thanks also to the editors and staffs of the following journals, anthologies, and institutions for publishing these poems, sometimes in earlier versions:

agape: "The Borrowed World," "Hart & Sword," "Pacific Cliffs," "A Question"

Best New Poets 2012: "Fidelity"

BLOOM: "Cock Fight," "July"

Boston Review, What Nature Poetry Forum: "A Dedication"

Copious Collaboration: "Childhood," set to music by Weston Brown

Dorothy Sargent Rosenberg Poetry Prizes 2010: "Childhood," "Möbius Strip"

Image: "Blod Aria"

Long Poem Magazine: "Love Song for the New World"

The Missouri Review: "Imbolc"

New Poetry from the Midwest 2019: "Cock Fight"

The Poetry Society of America Chapbook Anniversary: "Fidelity"

RHINO: "Hallucination with Four Fathers," "This Time Thistles"

Seattle Review: "Little Ochre Flame"

Wells College Press Broadside Series: "Hallucination with Four
   Fathers"

Windhover: "To a Future Self"

(B) = Winner of the Brittingham Prize in Poetry
(FP) = Winner of the Felix Pollak Prize in Poetry
(4L) = Winner of the Four Lakes Prize in Poetry

CHRISTOPHER NELSON

is the founder and editor of the journal *Under a Warm Green Linden* and Green Linden Press, a nonprofit publisher dedicated to reforestation. His chapbooks are *Blue House, Capital City at Midnight,* and *Love Song for the New World.* Among his honors are inclusion in the Best New Poets series and fellowships from the Poetry Society of America and the U.S. Department of Education. Visit christophernelson.info